Never Give Up

Four True Life Stories About
DETERMINATION

COVER ILLUSTRATION:

Justin Ray Thompson

PHOTO CREDITS:

Allsport USA—Tom Able-Green, p. 6
AP/Wide World—Michel Spingler, p. 8; Bill Janscha, p. 10; Richard Vogel, pp. 12, 16; Manish Swarup, p. 15; other: end pages (Jackie Robinson) & pp. 21, 22, 28
Archive Photos—p. 18
Granger Collection—pp. 24, 26

Visit us at *www.kidsbooks.com*

VALUES IN ACTION ™

Never Give Up

Four True Life Stories About
DETERMINATION

Determination is the ability to focus on a goal, even in the face of danger, fear, or other tough challenges. In this book, you will meet four extraordinary people who never gave up, despite great obstacles. Their determination to succeed earned them worldwide respect.

Lance Armstrong
by Denise Rinaldo

Aung San Suu Kyi
by Denise Rinaldo

Jackie Robinson
by Kathleen J. Edgar

Eleanor Roosevelt
by Kathleen J. Edgar

Lance Armstrong

born 1971

The year was 1996. Bicyclist Lance Armstrong was at the top of his game. He was about to be named one of the top five cyclists in the world. He had just signed a $2.5 million contract with a French bike-racing team, and had built himself a beautiful new house on a Texas lake. Life seemed perfect—until October 2 of that year. The 25-year-old cyclist learned that he had cancer that had spread to his abdomen, lungs, and brain. Doctors gave him only a 40-percent chance for survival. At first, Lance thought that his career—and life—were over. But drawing on the strength and determination that had made him a champion in the first place, he triumphed over the disease and emerged an even greater athlete.

Working Toward His Dreams

Lance Edward Armstrong was born on September 18, 1971, in Plano, Texas. He grew up there with his mother, Linda. Linda struggled to make ends meet through much of Lance's childhood. No matter how tough things got, though, she pushed Lance to finish what he started and to stay focused on his dreams. Lance, whose own determination to succeed was inspired by hers, has called Linda his hero.

Lance got his first bike when he was 7, and immediately fell in love with cycling. He was also a talented swimmer and runner. Soon, he began competing in triathlons—races that involve running, swimming,

Lance Armstrong, wearing the prestigious yellow jersey of the race's leader, cycles at the head of the U.S. team during 1999's Tour de France.

and cycling. When he was 13, he won the IronKids Triathlon, a national competition for young people.

In high school, Lance gave up running and swimming to concentrate on cycling. His senior year, he was invited to train with the U.S. Olympic developmental team in Colorado Springs, Colorado. The training schedule there was so tough that Lance came close to failing in school. In the late spring, however, he hired tutors and dedicated himself to his schoolwork. Lance's determination paid off: He graduated with his class.

At 19, Lance became the U.S. National Amateur Champion. In 1992, he signed a professional contract with Motorola, the only real U.S. cycling team at that time.

Lance's first professional competition was the 1992 Classico San Sebastian in Spain. He had high hopes for the race, but crossed the finish line last—almost a half-hour behind the winner. That loss, Lance has said, devastated him. He had thoughts of giving up, but remembered the example of hard work and determination set by his mother, and went back to work. Living in Italy, he trained as hard as he could, riding up and down steep mountain roads for hours at time. He rode in pouring rain and bitter cold. The following year, he won the world and U.S. professional championships, and a stage (section) of the Tour de France—the most famous bike race in the world. He also finished first in the San Sebastian race that he had lost the year before.

"If you ever get a second chance in life, you've got to go all the way."
—Lance Armstrong

For the next several years, Lance spent much of his time in Europe, where cycling is wildly popular. He set records and won races—and became the first cyclist to appear on the Wheaties cereal box, known for featuring top-notch athletes.

The Toughest Test of All

In 1996, Lance signed a two-year, $2.5 million contract with Cofidis, a French team. That same year, he began feeling weak. Finally, he went to a doctor—and learned that he was suffering from advanced cancer. Within days of the diagnosis, Lance had surgery. Soon afterward, he began chemotherapy (taking a series of powerful drugs) to kill any cancer cells left behind. Although the drugs made him feel very sick, Lance biked 30 to 50 miles a day throughout the months of treatment.

The treatments succeeded: Tests showed that he was cancer-free. In 1998, Lance married Kristin Richard. He also decided to return to racing, but his team, Cofidis, turned him away. Other famous teams rejected him, too, not believing that he could compete after all that he had been through. Then he signed with the U.S. Postal Service's pro cycling team. After a slow start, Lance astonished the cycling world by becoming an even greater rider than he was before. He won race after race. In 1999, he won the big one: the Tour de France. People were amazed that

After winning the 2001 Tour de France, Lance Armstrong—with his wife Kristin and their son Luke—was honored by President George W. Bush.

Tour de France

The Tour de France is one of the most challenging athletic events ever. Held every July since 1903, the three-week race covers more than 2,000 miles, up and down the Alps and Pyrenees mountains, and through farms and scenic towns.

Each day of the race, called a "stage," begins in one town and ends in another. Cycling fans from around the world line the streets, wildly cheering their favorite riders. Each day's leading cyclist gets to wear a yellow jersey the next day. The winner is the cyclist who crosses the finish line in Paris with the lowest overall time.

In 2001, Lance Armstrong did it in 86 hours, 17 minutes, 28 seconds. He gave the $285,000 prize to his team, as thanks for their help.

a man who had so recently come close to death could triumph in this grueling competition. Later that year, Kristin and Lance had another triumph—a baby boy, Luke.

After that, Lance seemed to have nowhere to go but up. He won the Tour de France again in 2000 and 2001, making him the only American to win the race three years in a row.

Lance says that he is just getting started and will win many more races. He also says that his battle with cancer taught him a priceless lesson in determination. "It made me a tougher and more patient cyclist," he has said, "and I think I'm also a better person overall because of it—more thoughtful, more compassionate, and more responsible."

Life Lines

1971 Lance Edward Armstrong is born in Plano, Texas, on September 18.

1984 Lance wins the IronKids Triathlon.

1991 Lance wins the U.S. amateur cycling title.

1992 Lance competes in the Olympic Games in Barcelona, Spain, then becomes a professional cyclist.

1996 Lance signs a $2.5 million contract with the Cofidis team. In October, he learns that he has cancer and starts chemotherapy.

1997 Lance establishes the Lance Armstrong Foundation to fund cancer research and help cancer victims.

1999 A year after returning to professional cycling, Lance wins the Tour de France. He wins it again in 2000 and 2001.

Aung San Suu Kyi

born 1945

Aung San Suu Kyi's life goal is to bring democracy to the Southeast Asian country of Myanmar, also called Burma. The country's brutal military government has tried to block her at every turn. It has threatened her with death, locked her up under house arrest, and barred her from seeing her husband and two sons. No matter what is done to her, Aung San Suu Kyi *(ong sahn soo chee)* refuses to back down. In honor of her determination and spirit, she was awarded the Nobel Peace Prize in 1991.

Like Father, Like Daughter

Suu was born on June 19, 1945, in Rangoon, Burma (now Yangon, Myanmar). As a little girl, she loved listening to stories about her father. A heroic and dashing man, General Aung San had dedicated himself to uniting the people in a democratic Burma. Political opponents killed him when Suu was only two years old. To this day, he is a national hero to many Burmese. Suu's mother, Khin Kyi, was also a distinguished person in Burmese politics. She worked for many years as a diplomat.

Suu dreamed of someday continuing her father's struggle, but took an indirect route to that goal. She studied philosophy and politics at Oxford University in England and worked for the United Nations in New York. In 1972, she married Michael Aris, a British scholar. For 16 years, Suu was a wife and mother, living in England with Michael and their sons, Alexander and Kim. Then, everything changed.

> *"It is not enough merely to call for freedom, democracy, and human rights. There has to be a united determination to persevere in the struggle."*
> —Aung San Suu Kyi

In 1988, Suu's mother suffered a stroke. Suu rushed to Burma to be with her. At that time, the country was in turmoil. Huge protests had broken out against a dictatorship that had been trampling on people's rights and ruining the economy. Government soldiers fired on the crowds, killing thousands of civilians. Thousands more were being imprisoned. Suu watched this in horror. When protest leaders called on her to help, she did what she could. On August 26, 1988, she made her first public appearance, speaking to a rally of a half-million people.

Devotion to a Cause

Standing beneath a huge poster of her father, Suu urged the protesters to stay strong and never resort to violence. They were energized by the speech and thrilled to see Suu—truly her father's daughter—take a stand. From that day on, she was the leader of her homeland's democracy movement. She was determined to stay there and work to make a difference. Her husband and sons returned to England, but planned to visit often.

Suu crisscrossed the country, making speeches. Once, she faced down gun-toting soldiers trying to stop her from campaigning with the political party she helped found, the National League for Democracy (NLD). The government, which disapproved of Suu's political activities, put her under house arrest and cut her phone lines. Soon—when Alexander was 16 and Kim 12—the government banned Suu's family from entering the country.

International pressure forced the government to hold elections in 1990. The NLD won in a landslide, but was never allowed to take office.

During Suu's captivity, she showed great courage and determination. She made posters about democracy and hung them on her fence. She smuggled out her writings whenever she could. The military offered her food, but she refused to accept anything from them, so she often suffered from malnutrition.

Suu's only knowledge of the outside world came through a small radio she was allowed to keep, but the world knew about her. More and more newspapers and magazines were writing about her courage. Her story brought her country's plight to the attention of the world. In 1991, she

On Women's Day in June 2001, these marchers in New Delhi, India, honored Aung San Suu Kyi.

Suu's Homeland

Name:
Myanmar *(MYAHN-mar)*; before 1989, it was known by its English name, Burma

Capital:
Yangon (formerly Rangoon)

Population (2001 estimate):
48 million (about one third aged 15 or under)

Political background:
Decades of repressive rule have made Myanmar a poor, freedom-starved nation. The military government spends only about 30 cents a year per student on education. (By contrast, the U.S. government spends about $7,000 a year per student.) Four of every 10 children are malnourished.

In Myanmar, it is illegal to use a cell phone or own a fax machine, because government leaders fear that people will use them to plan protests. Tens of thousands of the people have fled from their homes to escape abuse by government troops.

Aung San Suu Kyi believes that a democratic government would allow people freedom, and would work to solve their economic problems.

won the Nobel Peace Prize, awarded to a person who has made extraordinary efforts to advance the causes of peace and justice. Suu heard about the prize on the radio, but was not allowed to go to Sweden to accept it. Her sons accepted it for her.

In July 1995, Suu was released from house arrest. She went back to making speeches, organizing for democracy, and helping the poor. Then, in 1998, she was faced with a terrible choice. Her husband, Michael Aris, was dying of cancer, and

Aung San Suu Kyi with a portrait of her famous father, General Aung San

asked Myanmar's government to let him into the country to see Suu one last time. The government refused, saying that Suu should go to England to be with him. Suu knew that if she left the country, she would never be allowed back to continue her work, so she chose to stay in Myanmar. Michael died on March 27, 1999.

Since Suu's 1995 release, she has been re-arrested and confined to her home several more times. At other times, though, the government has entered into talks and has released some political prisoners. Suu believes that if she and her allies keep the pressure on, her homeland will one day be a free and democratic nation. "Unless my lifetime is unexpectedly short," she says, "I certainly will see democracy come to Burma."

Life Lines

1945 Aung San Suu Kyi is born in Rangoon, Burma, on June 19.

1947 On July 19, Suu's father, General Aung San, is assassinated by political enemies.

1988 Suu, who has been living in England with her husband and sons, returns to Burma to care for her sick mother. While there, Suu becomes a leader in the nation's struggle for democracy.

1989 Suu is placed under house arrest.

1991 Suu wins the Nobel Peace Prize. Her sons accept it for her.

1995 Myanmar's military government releases Suu from house arrest; however, it has rearrested her several times since.

2000 President Bill Clinton awards Suu the Presidential Medal of Freedom, the highest civilian honor in the U.S.

Jackie Robinson

born 1919 • died 1972

April 15, 1947, when Jackie Robinson took the field for the Brooklyn Dodgers, was an important day for baseball. It also marked a new era in U.S. history. Jackie became the first African American to play major-league baseball in the 20th century. Being first was extremely difficult: Jackie's every move, on and off the field, was watched. All that season, he stepped up to the plate, enduring the pressure of cruel insults and even death threats. Eventually, his talent—and dignity—earned him the respect of fans and other ballplayers. Through his determination to succeed, Jackie opened doors for African Americans in many professions.

Against the Odds

When Jack Roosevelt Robinson was born on January 31, 1919, in Cairo, Georgia, the United States was deeply divided by race. In some parts of the country, particularly the South, segregation (separation by race) was widely practiced. Sometimes by tradition, sometimes by law, whites and blacks were kept apart. They attended separate schools and sat in separate areas of restaurants, trains, buses, and movie theaters. They even used separate water fountains. Baseball, too, was segregated. The major leagues were for white athletes only; black athletes played in the Negro League.

Jackie's parents were sharecroppers—poor farmers in the South. After his father left the family, Jackie's mother moved her five children

The Other Pioneer

Jackie Robinson's barrier-breaking achievement was not a solo act. It also took the courage and determination of Branch Rickey, president of the Brooklyn Dodgers.

White club owners had a "gentleman's agreement" to keep baseball segregated, but Branch Rickey wanted the best players, regardless of race. He knew that the man he picked to be first had to be the right man.

"Jackie," he warned, "we've got no army. There's virtually nobody on our side. No owners, no umpires, very few newspapermen. And I'm afraid that many fans may be hostile. . . . We can win only if we can convince the world that I am doing this because you're a great ballplayer and a fine gentleman." Branch Rickey chose the right man for the job.

to Pasadena, California. Racism was part of life there, too, but Jackie refused to be held back by it. He developed inner strength and a drive to succeed.

In high school and college, Jackie excelled in sports, including basketball, football, track, and baseball. He was the first athlete to receive four varsity letters at the University of California-Los Angeles (UCLA). While there, he met Rachel Issum, who later became his wife. The couple eventually had three children.

During World War II, Jackie served in the U.S. Army, rising to the rank of second lieutenant. As a soldier, he again experienced racism, but refused to accept unfair treatment. After the war in 1945, Jackie decided to play baseball for a living. Like many other gifted African Americans, Jackie was shut out from the majors, so he joined a Negro League team, the Kansas City Monarchs, in 1945.

The "Great Experiment"

After World War II, some Americans wanted to integrate baseball. Branch Rickey, president of the Brooklyn Dodgers, was one of them. He decided to try what he called baseball's "great experiment." He would force a change and integrate the majors by hiring a black player for his team. Branch Rickey chose carefully, looking for a man who had experience playing on integrated teams in college, was even-tempered, and could withstand racial slurs.

Jackie Robinson fit the bill. Not only had he attended a mainly white college and played integrated baseball there, he had proven his patriotism in the Army. Although Jackie had not played long in the Negro League and was not its best player, Branch Rickey believed that Jackie was the best candidate to cross baseball's color barrier. Jackie and Branch both knew that many white owners, players, and fans would resist integration, but both believed that it was time for change.

> *"Life is not a spectator sport. . . . If you're going to spend your whole life in the grandstand just watching what goes on, in my opinion you're wasting your life."*
> —Jackie Robinson

A historic moment: Jackie Robinson and Branch Rickey sign Jackie's major-league contract.

Jackie Robinson in action, sliding in under a tag

In late 1945, Jackie signed with the Dodgers' minor-league team in Montreal, Canada, and played well there. In 1947, at age 28, he was called up for major-league duty. Vicious racial insults were hurled at him from dugouts and stands, and by some reporters, but Jackie was determined to ignore them. He kept cool in the face of overwhelming pressure, including death threats, because he knew that his success would create opportunities for other black athletes. "I'm not concerned with your liking or disliking me," he once said. "All I ask is that you respect me as a human being."

On the playing field, Jackie let his talent speak for him. His batting, fielding, and base stealing—including dramatic slides across home plate—gradually won over many of the people who had opposed him. At the end of Jackie's first season, he was named the National League's first Rookie of the Year. His success led other teams to hire African American athletes. The successful integration of major-league baseball had begun.

During Jackie's 10 seasons with the Dodgers, they won the National League (NL) pennant six times and the World Series once. In 1949, he won the NL's batting title and was named its Most Valuable Player (MVP).

Jackie continued to cross barriers. After retiring from baseball in early 1957, he became a vice president of a major corporation, and later began a construction company to help low-income families. He died in 1972, 10 years after being inducted into the National Baseball Hall of Fame. In 1997, the 50th anniversary of his breaking baseball's color barrier, Major League Baseball (MLB) retired his number, 42, throughout the major leagues. It was the only time a player has been so honored.

Jackie Robinson's great personal strength, talent, dignity, and determination forever changed the face of baseball—and the nation. Today, long after his feats on the playing field, we remember his name and honor his achievements.

Life Lines

1919 Jack Roosevelt Robinson is born in Cairo, Georgia, on January 31.

1942-1945 Jackie serves in the U.S. Army.

1947 Jackie crosses major-league baseball's color barrier and becomes the first National League Rookie of the Year.

1949 Jackie's .342 average earns him the NL batting title. He also wins the NL's Most Valuable Player award.

1957 Jackie retires from baseball after 10 seasons as a Dodger.

1962 Jackie is inducted into the Baseball Hall of Fame.

1972 Jackie's autobiography, *I Never Had It Made*, is published. Jackie Robinson dies in Stamford, Connecticut, on October 24.

1999 Jackie Robinson is named to the MLB All-Century Team.

Eleanor Roosevelt

born 1884 • died 1962

As a child, Eleanor Roosevelt was shy, awkward, and plain, and sometimes felt unloved. Despite her troubles, she developed a great determination to help others and became a supporter of equal, civil, and human rights. The daughter of wealthy parents and the niece of President Theodore Roosevelt, Eleanor led a life of privilege, but did not ignore the social problems she saw. When her husband, Franklin Delano Roosevelt, became president, she found herself in a position to make a difference. Ultimately, Eleanor Roosevelt became one of the most distinguished, beloved, and respected women in the world—a champion of human rights worldwide.

Getting Political

When Anna Eleanor Roosevelt was born on October 11, 1884, in New York City, most American women could not vote. (Only a few states allowed it, for local elections only.) Few women worked outside the home and those who did worked long hours for little pay. The children of needy families worked, too, often in harsh sweatshop conditions. Racial discrimination against African Americans and immigrants was widespread.

During childhood, Eleanor struggled with her looks. Her mother, who was a great beauty, made Eleanor feel plain. Both parents died before Eleanor turned 10. She went to live with her grandmother, who eventually sent her to school in England. There, Eleanor became pop-

Eleanor Roosevelt proudly holds a copy of the Universal Declaration of Human Rights. She played a major role in getting it drafted and adopted by the United Nations.

ular and gained self-esteem. While in England, she also learned about social problems and became determined to do something about them.

Eleanor returned to New York in 1902. Three years later, she married Franklin Delano Roosevelt, a wealthy young law student. Eleanor and Franklin shared an interest in helping others.

In 1910, Franklin was elected to the New York state senate as a Democrat. Eleanor busied herself raising their children. (They eventually had six.) Then, in 1921, Franklin was stricken with polio, a serious illness that made walking difficult. He considered giving up politics, but Eleanor was determined to help him continue. Franklin required a wheelchair or crutches, so Eleanor traveled to places that he could not, acting as his eyes and ears. Though political opponents mocked her, many people respected her. Eleanor's work helped Franklin become governor of New York in 1929 and president of the United States in 1933.

So Much to Do

Eleanor didn't hold office, but she had political smarts—and power. She used them to support various social causes, particularly those involving women's rights, racial discrimination, children, and the poor. As First Lady of the U.S., she held press conferences for female reporters only, which encouraged newspapers to employ at least one female journalist. Eleanor wrote articles, too. She continued to travel throughout the country and abroad, reporting back to Franklin.

When Eleanor spoke out about an issue, it got national attention. Equality was a controversial cause at that time, but she never backed down in her support of it. In 1937, for instance, she refused to give a speech for a club that excluded Jews. She made another news splash in 1939, when she took a stand against the Daughters of the American Revolution (DAR), a prestigious, all-white women's group. The DAR had refused to allow Marian Anderson, a famous black singer, to perform at Constitution Hall. Eleanor, a longtime DAR member, withdrew from the group in protest. She then used her government connections to secure a new site for Anderson's concert: the Lincoln Memorial in Washington, D.C.

Franklin was elected to four terms as president (the only U.S. president to do so). During his time in office, the nation faced two crises: the Great Depression and World War II. To combat the severe economic problems of the Depression, Franklin created work

"You gain strength, courage, and confidence by every experience in which you really stop to look fear in the face. You are able to say to yourself, 'I lived through this horror. I can take the next thing that comes along.' . . . You must do the thing you think you cannot do."

—Eleanor Roosevelt

The First Lady with Madame Chiang Kai-shek, wife of a Chinese leader.

and assistance programs. Many of his decisions were based, at least in part, on observations made by Eleanor as she crisscrossed the country on his behalf. During the war, she continued her travels, speeches, writings, and social-reform work. Named assistant director of the Office of Civilian Defense in 1941, she traveled to war-torn Great Britain in 1942, learning how British women aided their country's defense. She also visited hundreds of thousands of U.S. soldiers at home and abroad, boosting their spirits and listening to their concerns.

Rights for All

Eleanor Roosevelt worked hard to get world leaders to accept the Universal Declaration of Human Rights.

That document, adopted by the United Nations in 1948, outlines basic civil and political rights for people world-wide. It was drafted just after World War II, in an era when millions of innocent people had been killed by ruthless governments, and countless other lives were being lost to poverty, hunger, and political uprisings.

Today, the principles of the Universal Declaration of Human Rights remain important as the UN and other aid organizations strive to make a difference wherever people suffer from hunger, political persecution, or ethnic strife.

On April 12, 1945, Franklin died in office. As the nation mourned, Eleanor told the press, "The story is over." It wasn't. Eleanor soon regained her political drive and worked on social causes until her death in 1962. Notably, she served as chairperson of the United Nations Human Rights Commission and began work on a Universal Declaration of Human Rights, which was adopted by the UN in 1948.

Capable, intelligent, and charming, Eleanor Roosevelt never stopped working to improve the lives of others around the world. Though often ridiculed and controversial, she was widely respected for her caring, toughness, and determination. After her death on November 7, 1962, U.S. flags were flown at half-staff in her honor.

Life Lines

1884 Anna Eleanor Roosevelt is born in New York City on October 11.

1921 Eleanor's husband, Franklin, is stricken with polio.

1933 Franklin Delano Roosevelt becomes the 32nd president of the United States. Eleanor continues as his political helpmate.

1941 Eleanor is named assistant director of the Office of Civilian Defense.

1945 Franklin dies in office. The new president, Harry Truman, appoints Eleanor a U.S. delegate to the United Nations (UN).

1948 The UN adopts the Universal Declaration of Human Rights.

1961 President John F. Kennedy appoints Eleanor first chairperson of the President's Commission on the Status of Women.

1962 Eleanor dies in New York City on November 7.